LOVE DIARY
OF A YOUNG POET

AHLA IQBAL

To the light that sparkled my eyes...

Contents

Contents

Foreword

Dear reader,

Love Diary of a Young Poet is a romantic recollection in verse written by my dear student, Ahla Iqbal. A poetic manifesto of a girl longing for love through symbolisms and imageries drawn from nature. A book that heals our psyche, soothes, and calms our soul and transports readers to an ecstatic realm of love.

The collection offers a testament on the universal theme of love, capturing its nuances with grace and precision. These poems will touch your heart and awaken your senses through introspective and thought -provoking lines. The poet has been able to capture the real feelings and meanings what someone may feel once they are in love.

The book is a celebration of the power of love and the limitless potential of the written word. As a teacher, I am constantly in awe of the creativity and passion that my student brings through her writing. Uniqueness of the anthology lies in its interconnected verses and the ways in which it intersects with our lives.

I am so proud of my student's hard work and dedication in creating this anthology, which holds the power of love to inspire and lift us all. I hope that this collection will touch your heart and leave you with a deeper appreciation for the love that surrounds us.

Dr Reshmi S

Preface

This book is a collection of romantic poems that is dedicated to a lover. One could experience the love story of a young girl portrayed through these poems; A Long Stare, Love Stamp, Into Those Eyes, In Love With.....?, Love Is Born, Into Him, How Can I Define My Love, Unrequited Love Is Pain, Everlasting Love, Love, Laugh in Pain, For You, A Little Of Me, Love From The Clouds, Undefinable, Take Me Then Grab Me, Hey it's Time, Lovely Drop, Lullaby Of Waves, Possible, The Way She Fell For Him, You're The....., Let It Be and Dedication.

Every beautiful soul in this world might have a symbol for their love. Poetry is the signature of a poet and this book of book is the symbol of love of a loving soul who is a poet.

- Love Diary,

Of a young poet.

Acknowledgements

" To be yourself in a world that is constantly trying to make you something else is the greatest accomplishment".

-Ralph Waldo Emerson

Thanks to all my beloveds for being with me. Above all thanks to the Almighty!

Prologue

Look,

she's in hurry..

for what?

To find her love,

to hold it tightly,

&

to endure it!

1. The Long Stare

That was a long stare…
a very deep one
that penetrated into
my soul.
I was not aware
enough
of how it might
turns to be, purposely
I had left
it there, alone,
how come I could
know it's value
when I was all alone
searching for something
that doesn't suit me,
despite of being an
outcast at that time
it became a part of
me, and started to
grow with me.

2. Love Stamp

Found the stare that
stamped my soul
at many places,
it was so easy for me
to discover those eyes,
looking at me.
Became a hobby for me
to search those eyes,
once I left unnoticed.
The effect it had on
me was so great,
that it made me sober.
My eyes, my soul
and everything
in me searched
for those eyes.
Then I realized that those
eyes had stamped,
a stamp of love
& it was the cause
for
the longest stare.

3. Into Those Eyes

I dreamed of getting
lost in those eyes
once again with
all my heart,
now with more
love and care,
to flourish him,
his eyes & the
untold love
of mine.
I took vibrant steps
to get locked in him,
it took only
a moment to
as I had
got a deep connection
with him from the
meeting of ours.
Stared, blinked &
looked into him helplessly,
as I couldn't help
me to get closer to him
but to look from a long distance.

4. In Love With...?

In love with whom?
i asked myself
in the middle of night, i found
nothing but
something that i can't
explain, only could feel
it, all by myself.
Opened my eyes
with his thoughts,
and closed it
with the same.
I wasn't aware of
my doings
it might be either good or
the best for me
i always thought the best
about him.
This love will, with all its
imperfections
stays with me.

5. Love Is Born

Yess, the moment had come
to love and to cherish its beauty.
Love is in the every
parts of mine.
When a love is born
we may feel that
we too are born.
We could feel its freshness
and it will not be lost
at any time.
As for a love there's
no end,
love is not the same for
everyone,
it differs
and that's the
uniqueness of love,
we all are unique
thus the
love
is.

6. Into Him

I started to love him more
but the inability to express
hurts me.
I kept it so close
to myself/ within me.
I thought it might lose its beauty
when expressed
so, I kept it with utmost
love & care,
I looked at him
as he passed,
he smiled at me
so lovely, I stood there
like an angel
with all love that could bloom the world..
I too have a tale of love
to tell the whole world.
If you ask me what kind it is
I'm afraid that I
couldn't answer you
as my love is
undefinable!

7. How Can I Define My Love

On my way to let him
feel what's in my heart,
I got confused of the
way I should,
I thought about it but
I got nothing
I don't know how to
express it loudly
but I got the magic
to let it live in me
without any distortions
I couldn't find any words
that could suit
the meaning of love,
love is not simple
to explain
the only way is to feel it.

8. Unrequited Love is Pain

We may tremble to breathe
when we're denied the love
of whom we love the most.
I too trembled for the
unrequited love of mine,
but I felt that I
might be living in the other side
with all his love,
I will never stop loving
and I believe that
one day it will come to me
I saw him walking then I
asked myself that
when I will be able to hold
those hands
I smiled in tears.
Was that a joy?
NOO
that was a painful joy.

9. Everlasting Love

My love always chose to
hide so that no
one could touch it/defile,
but I wished if it could
be visible to him,
wasn't he unable to
read my eyes,
as it had always reflected my love.
It doesn't matter as
long as it stays in me,
I don't want to
let it fade simply
I want to let it grow
with me
as days are getting passed
it gets intensified
more than before.
For my love, there
is no end or destiny
as those things that
has its own destiny would
someday meet its end.

10. Love

When all my thoughts
are filled by him,
what could I do?
what should I do if
I couldn't stop me
from loving
him,
will the law of nature
unites us?
I'm here waiting for him
to love me &
I don't want to lose it
how can I let it go
when the other end is
so beautiful,
in actual that's not an end,
my love has no end
I'm here waiting for him
to love me.

11. Laugh In Pain

When I speak and
when I write my
heart is in pain
I couldn't even fake a
smile,
I'm not able to
conceal it
that's the reality
you let me and
made me
the real,
even though my heart is in pain
I could endure it
as my love is much
stronger than the
pain.

12. For You

Give me a chance, for
me to express to you
my love
I'm here with all my
love
with no scars on it
waiting for you,
to bid.
I would come closer
to you after some months
or years
then I could get myself
glued to your soul
I just want you to feel
my love
I'm living here with a
hope that one day
you will do the same.

13. A Little Of Me

I walked away whenever I saw you
but the inner me echoed loudly
to run towards you.
I swear, I was so helpless
as I felt something that held
me back & that was not
simple as it seems, it felt like
I was reduced into an invisible thing..
I cried & cried & cried
and became more intense
as the days got passed..
Those tears carried a little
of my love, that goes
like an air to reach you,
then to touch you
so, you could know or experience
what I feel.
Will you let it go?
Will you let go of something
that went a long way
to reach you.

14. Love From The Clouds

You may ask me
How I breathe even in
the midst of mystery,
you may sing
some lyrics to me
when I'm all stuck
in the blues,
what should I do
or how can I
so that you may
do all these for me.
But there came
something that is
mysterious
down from the clouds
to soothe me.
What was that?
you might think
but I can't serve you
as I want it to be
hidden in me
as the same mysterious

thing that no one
touch nor
louse up!

• 15 •

15. Undefinable

How much does it
cost to wait a long time?
I asked myself
but it seems to be
something that couldn't
be given such
price tags.
I had heard a lot
and read a lot
about love longings,
so, I was just
wondering how it might look,
would it make our
soul disfigured or
an exquisite one?
I'd thought how the ones
in love would feel
and what would be
the difference in views &
how their eyes look into
this world.
And I wished that if I
could witness too,

my mind was full of

such thoughts.

Even though I did get nothing but

i got to knew that love is something undefinable, thus the

one in love.

16. Take Me Then Grab Me

Take me into your eyes
so that I could live
more & more in your eyes,
it feels like I'm
more into you
to live in your heart.
Grab me in your hands
whenever you could,
to let me not to
float in the pain that
could take me along.
Hold me into your chest
so covered in your fragrance
to let me taste the
power of care.

17. Hey It's Time

It's time to fall

in

love

with you

again and again in

all the ways

possible,

i wish to be

with you there near

the skies

so far.

Darling, love me at

the sky

between the clouds,

let me float with

you along with

the clouds..

18. Lovely Drops

While it was raining
i watched how those
drops falls into
the very heart of earth
i knew that it reflected me,
then, i thought to myself
that how beautiful
it is to fall for
someone, like the raindrops.
Even if they are penetrated deep into
the soil, it never stops
i adored myself for this
and those lovely drops.
Was it because of you that
i could realize
how beautiful
might be
me falling for
you..

19. Lullaby Of Waves

The love waves lulled

something to me,

about you,

me,

and about us.

The waves got raised

to the clouds

then,

hugged me,

to take all my

worries away,

madly i got

drowned into

this very moment.

remembrance of you

whenever i

approached

those waves

soothed me.

Wished for this

to happen

again

and

again..
Would there be a day where we
could witness together?
The love waves lulled
something to me,
about you,
me,
and about us.
The waves got raised
to the clouds
then,
hugged me,
to take all my
worries away,
madly i got
drowned into
this very moment.
remembrance of you
whenever i
approached
those waves
soothed me.
Wished for this
to happen
again
and
again..

Would there be a day where we
could witness together?-v-v-vv-

20. Possible

When the thought of
you arrives,
my fingers would
float to find
the papers and pen
to let it come
through the
words that
comes from me,
but the words are
so insufficient for
me to describe
my love for you,
my hands would shake
out of my sorrow
then, there comes
my tear drops
to accompany.
Even though we are not
possible now
i could make it
in my poems.

21. The Way She Falls For Him

I love to get lost in your eyes
so that i could see myself in
you
your eyes reflect my love for
you then,
i got lost in your eyes again &
again,
when i see you my pupil
contracts,
when i walk away my feet got
paralyzed,
it's your soul that makes me
stuck
when i touch you a ray of love
passes me & makes me
lovelier,
when i hug you everything
besides me
rises up to see my love for you.
Then you may hold me tighter
& make others envy about
us.

LOVE DIARY

As i got lost in love
i couldn't move away.

22. You're The.....

You are the leonides that
i see in my dreams
and the one besides me
when it snows.
You are the one who sees
me in my gloomy days
when i was all stuck
in the midst of grey.
You are the wind that
passes through my hair
then i felt the warmth
of you in me.
You may please hold my hands as
I'm getting drowned in the vein of thoughts.

23. Let It Be!

I have kept you in my heart
& You were there in me every time,
i blushed so lovely when we
met in my eyes.
The thought of you strikes me
so hardly when i imagined
that we would never meet.
Why i loved you this much, i asked
myself, but now i can't unlove,
my heart can't beat so good as
you're not here with me,
i would never let the
love to fade & i would always keep
it so close to me,
as i am not able to express
my mind you can't see my love,
i don't know what to do
the only thing that i know is
to only love you.
Please let me be yours,
i would never let you
go fade, i can be your only moon
& i wish to be,

i wish to be your hope &

i want to hold your love.

When my desire is so hard that it would come true!

• 29 •

24. Dedication

To the light that sparkled my eyes
I'm sharing a part of my love
for you through my words.
Days are passing and here I'm
unable to express
with no one to hear.
It feels like the world is
moving apart whenever i saw you
and becoming blurred then,
all i could see is YOU!
A book of love by ME for YOU.